Ever
of 19__

News for every day of the year

The Duke and Duchess of York, later Their Majesties King George VI and Queen Elizabeth (the Queen Mother), are married on 26 April 1923.

By Hugh Morrison

MONTPELIER PUBLISHING

Front cover (clockwise from left): The Charleston dance craze begins on 29 October. The formation of Imperial Airways is announced on 17 December. *Time* magazine is first published on 3 March. Julius the Cat, one of the characters of the new Walt Disney company founded on 16 October. Harold Lloyd stars in the comedy *Safety Last*, released on 1 April.

Back cover (clockwise from top): Noel Coward: his new play *London Calling* opens on 4 September. Charlie Chaplin: his film *A Woman of Paris* is released on 26 September. Cutty Sark whisky is launched on 23 March. Howard Carter opens King Tutankhamun's tomb on 16 March. Soviet leader Lenin gives up power on 9 March. A participant in the first 24 Hours of Le Mans motor race on 26 May. Cecil B De Mille's film *The Ten Commandments* is released on 4 December.

Image credits: Albert Witzel, Paul Regnier, Bernard Gotfryd, GJ Raymond and Co.

Published in Great Britain by Montpelier Publishing.
Printed and distributed by Amazon KDP.

ISBN: 9798837415050

January
1923

Monday 1: All British railways are grouped into the 'Big Four' (LMS, LNER, GWR, SR) as the Railways Act 1921 goes into effect.

Tuesday 2: An Allied conference on German war reparations begins in Paris.

Wednesday 3: Buckingham Palace quashes rumours that Edward, Prince of Wales, is engaged to marry Princess Yolanda of Savoy.

HRH Edward, Prince of Wales.

Thursday 4: The Allied war reparations conference in Paris ends without agreement.

Friday 5: French aircraft are sighted over the Ruhr region of Germany as rumours spread that France is about to occupy the area.

Saturday 6: The US Senate votes to withdraw its troops occupying Germany's Rhineland region.

Sunday 7: The town of Rosewood, Florida, is burnt to the ground following six days of race riots.

January 1923

Monday 8: An Anglo-American conference opens in Washington, DC, to discuss the repayment of British war debt to the USA.

The first radio broadcast on location takes place, as the BBC transmits a production of *The Magic Flute* from the Royal Opera House, Covent Garden.

Tuesday 9: Following one of the most sensational trials of the 1920s, Edith Thompson and Frederick Bywaters are hanged at 9.00 am in London's Holloway and Pentonville prisons respectively, for the joint murder of Thompson's husband Percy in a crime of passion.

King Constantine of Greece dies on 11 January.

Wednesday 10: An uprising takes place in the territory of Klaipeda (between Germany and Lithuania) in protest over French occupation following a League of Nations mandate. The area is ultimately ceded to Lithuanian control.

Thursday 11: French and Belgian troops occupy the Ruhr region of Germany in response to Germany's default on war reparations payments.

King Constantine I of Greece dies aged 54.

Friday 12: The Grand Council of Fascism is established in Italy, under the rule of Benito Mussolini.

Left: French troops challenge a German civilian as they occupy the Ruhr on 11 January.

Above: a Cierva Autogyro seen from the ground. The prototype helicopter first flies on 17 January.

Saturday 13: The German government announces a campaign of passive resistance to the Franco-Belgian occupation of the Ruhr.

Sunday 14: The Soviet Union formally condemns the occupation of the Ruhr.

Monday 15: A German civilian is shot dead by French troops during protests over the Ruhr occupation.

Silent star Wallace Reid dies on 18 January.

Tuesday 16: The industrialist Harry Ford Sinclair spends three hours testifying in the ongoing Teapot Dome Oil Lease case, a US government corruption scandal.

Wednesday 17: A prototype helicopter or autogyro is first flown, by inventor Juan de la Cierva near Madrid, Spain.

Thursday 18: The silent film star and racing driver Wallace Reid dies aged 31 following a train accident.

Hyperinflation begins in Germany, with the Mark increasing from 9000 to the US dollar on January 1, to 23,800.

Friday 19: The German government orders all state employees to refuse co-operate with occupying French troops. Miners in Buer go on strike and all banking activity in Düsseldorf is halted.

Saturday 20: The country and western singer Slim Whitman is born in Tampa, Florida (died 2013).

January 1923

Buster Keaton and Phyllis Haver in *The Balloonatic*.

Sunday 21: The first coins bearing fascist symbols are authorised in Italy.

Monday 22: The comedy film *The Balloonatic* starring Buster Keaton is released.

Tuesday 23: The French government announces plans to cut off the occupied Ruhr region from the rest of Germany.

Wednesday 24: American troops withdraw from the Rhineland.

In the occupied Ruhr, rioting breaks out in Mainz after French authorities impose large fines on mines which refuse to give up their coal in lieu of war reparations.

Thursday 25: A general strike begins in the Ruhr.

Friday 26: The branch of the IRA (Irish Republican Army) opposed to the Free State compromise with Britain, announces it will burn down the houses of Free State Senate members.

Famous birthdays: country singer Slim Whitman (far left) is born on 20 January; author Norman Mailer is born on 31 January .

Above: Herma Szabo of Austria wins the World Figure Skating Championships on 28 January.

Saturday 27: The first German Nazi Party congress is held in Munich, with 6000 attendees.

Sunday 28: Fritz Kachler and Herma Szabo of Austria win the World Figure Skating Championships held in Vienna, Austria.

Monday 29: The Turkish leader Mustafa Kamal Pasha ('Ataturk') marries Latife Ussaki.

Tuesday 30: The Lausanne Convention is signed, stipulating the exchange of Christian and Muslim populations between Greece and Turkey following the end of the Greco-Turkish War.

Wednesday 31: The writer Norman Mailer (*The Naked and the Dead*) is born in Long Branch, New Jersey (died 2007).

February
1923

Thursday 1: 14 people are reported killed in clashes between troops and protestors in Mexico following an attempt by the army to put down a tram drivers' strike.

Above: Bill Ponsford makes a record 429 runs on 5 February.

Friday 2: A failed assassination attempt is made on Aleksander Stamboliyski, Prime Minister of Bulgaria.

Saturday 3: An 8.5 magnitude earthquake hits the Kamchatka Peninsula in the Soviet Union.

Sunday 4: French troops expand their occupation of Germany to include the regions of Offenburg and Appenweier.

Monday 5: The Australian cricketer Bill Ponsford MBE makes a record 429 runs after eight hours in a Victoria v Tasmania match in Melbourne.

Tuesday 6: Sir William Sefton Brancker, director of Britain's civil aviation authority, announces that within five years aeroplanes will travel between New York and London in 12 hours. The prediction does not come true until the 1960s.

Wednesday 7: George Lascelles, Earl of Harewood and director of the Royal Opera House, is born in London (died 2011).

The Central American Treaty of Peace and Amity is signed.

Thursday 8: A mine explosion in Dawson, New Mexico, kills 123; on the same day 33 miners die in a gas explosion at Cumberland, British Columbia.

The larger-than-life Irish writer Brendan Behan is born on 9 February.

Friday 9: Billy Hughes resigns as Prime Minister of Australia after failing to form a government; he is replaced by Stanley Bruce.

The Russian airline Aeroflot is founded.

The writer Brendan Behan (*Borstal Boy*) is born in Dublin (died 1964).

The silent comedy stars Harold Lloyd and Mildred Davis are married on 10 February.

Saturday 10: Silent film star Harold Lloyd marries Mildred Davis.

The German physicist Wilhelm Röntgen, discoverer of x-rays, dies aged 77.

Sunday 11: France and Belgium announce that all exports from the occupied Ruhr to the rest of Germany will be blocked.

Monday 12: The drama film *Jazzmania* is released.

The film and opera director Franco Zeffirelli is born in Florence, Italy (died 2019).

February 1923

Above: Tallulah Bankhead makes her London debut on 15 February.

Tuesday 13: Belgian troops block off the Ruhr from the Netherlands.

Chuck Yeager, first pilot to break the sound barrier, is born in Myra, West Virginia (died 2020).

Wednesday 14: The Dutch cargo ship *Lukkos* sinks in the English Channel with the loss of all hands.

Thursday 15: Actress Tallulah Bankhead makes her London stage debut in Gerald Du Maurier's play *The Dancers.*

Friday 16: The archaeologist Howard Carter opens the tomb of Tutankhamun in Luxor, Egypt.

Saturday 17: The BBC makes its first charitable appeal, for the Winter Distress League for homeless veterans.

Sunday 18: Olie Finerty and Edgar van Ollefin of Sunderland, England, set the world non-stop ballroom dancing record at 7 hours.

Above: Howard Carter opens the tomb of Egypt's King Tutankhamun on 16 February.

Monday 19: The US Supreme Court rules that persons of British Indian origin may not become American citizens. The ruling is in place until 1946.

Tuesday 20: Chamonix Mont Blanc in France is announced as the venue for the first ever Winter Olympics, to be held in 1924.

Wednesday 21: The birth control campaigner Marie Stopes sues medical author Dr Halliday Sutherland for libel after he calls her methods 'monstrous'. Stopes eventually loses the case.

Thursday 22: The International Save the Children Union adopts the Declaration of the Rights of the Child.

Friday 23: The last American troops leave Germany.

Boxer Gene Tunney retains the US Light-Heavyweight title on 23 February.

Gene Tunney beats Harry Greb to retake the American Light Heavyweight boxing title at Madison Square Garden, New York City.

Saturday 24: US President Warren G Harding expresses his desire for America to join the Permanent Court of International Justice (the World Court) but this is turned down on the grounds that it is too closely connected with the League of Nations.

Sunday 25: French troops extend their occupation of Germany to the cities of Kaub, Lorch and Konigswinter.

Above: Charlie Chaplin.

Monday 26: The Charlie Chaplin film *The Pilgrim* is released.

Tuesday 27: The BBC's first dance music programme is broadcast, featuring Marius B Winter and his band.

Wednesday 28: Britain's House of Lords debates the continuance of the requirement to show a passport when entering the UK. The system was introduced in 1914 to control entry of enemy aliens.

March
1923

Thursday 1: The actress Pola Negri announces she has broken off her engagement to comedian Charlie Chaplin because she is 'too poor.'

Friday 2: Pola Negri announces her engagement to Charlie Chaplin is back on; however, they never marry.

British explorer George Leigh Mallory departs for India to make his second attempt to climb Mount Everest. He goes missing on the mountain in June 1924 and his body is not found until 1999; it remains uncertain if he ever reached the summit.

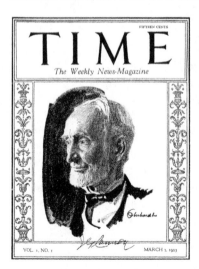

Saturday 3: The first issue of *Time* magazine is published; the cover shows US politician Joseph G Cannon.

Sunday 4: The astronomer Sir Patrick Moore is born in Pinner, Middlesex (died 2012).

Monday 5: The Soviet Union makes a formal protest to Finland over its claims to the border territory of Karelia.

Left: *Time* magazine is first published on 3 March.

Men in the news:

Far left: the future Prime Minister Neville Chamberlain becomes Britain's Minister of Health on 7 March.

Left: Soviet leader Vladimir Lenin suffers a major stroke on 9 March.

Tuesday 6: The Halibut Treaty on fishing rights is signed between the USA and Canada, the first Canadian treaty without a British intermediary.

Wednesday 7: Neville Chamberlain becomes Britain's Minister of Health.

Thursday 8: Buster Keaton's last short comedy film, *The Love Nest*, is released.

Friday 9: Soviet leader Vladimir Lenin suffers a major stroke, effectively ending his political career.

Saturday 10: The Spanish association football club Villareal is founded.

Sunday 11: 110 people with alleged links to the Irish Republican Army are rounded up across Britain and deported to Mountjoy Prison in Dublin.

Left: the film star Rudolph Valentino marries actress Natacha Rambova on 14 March.

March 1923

Monday 12: Seven people are killed in the Ruhr region of Germany after civilians clash with occupying French forces.

Tuesday 13: France announces a further 15,000 troops will be sent to the German Ruhr and Rhineland regions.

Wednesday 14: Film star Rudolf Valentino marries Natacha Rambova in Crown Point, Indiana.

The first ice hockey game broadcast on radio takes place in Canada between the Edmonton Eskimos and the Regina Capitals.

Thursday 15: Germany offers France 20 billion gold marks as part of a war reparations settlement to end the occupation of the Ruhr.

Friday 16: Paramount Picture's western film *The Covered Wagon* is released.

Saturday 17: US President Warren G Harding announces he will run again for election in 1924.

Above: the western film *The Covered Wagon* is released on 16 March.

Sunday 18: In an interview published in the *New York Times*, the British explorer George Mallory is asked why he wants to climb Mount Everest. 'Because it is there,' is his famous reply.

Monday 19: The 'Curse of Tutankhamun' strikes as Lord Carnavon becomes seriously ill with blood poisoning after open Tutankhamun's tomb; the cause is probably a mosquito bite.

Tuesday 20: The German government announces an unsupportable deficit of 7.1 trillion Marks.

Wednesday 21: The youngest known violators of the Volstead Act (Prohibition) are arrested in Hanford, California. Two nine year old boys are caught by their teacher in possession of a jug of wine; they refuse to tell police where they found it.

Thursday 22: *Phi Eta Sigma*, the first American university fraternity, is founded at the University of Michigan.

Friday 23: The Cutty Sark brand of whisky is introduced by Berry Brothers and Rudd.

'Sergeant Murphy' wins the Grand National.

Saturday 24: Oxford wins the 75th Boat Race.

3500 die in a 7.3 magnitude earthquake in Sichuan Province, China.

Sunday 25: The silent film version of William Makepeace Thackeray's novel *Vanity Fair* is released.

Cutty Sark whisky is launched on 23 March. It is aimed at the US contraband market.

The legendary French actress Sarah Bernhardt (shown here in 1864) dies on 26 March.

Monday 26: A farm labourers' strike begins in England after wages are cut from 25/- (£1.25) to 20/- (£1.00) per week.

The French actress Sarah Bernhardt dies aged 78.

Tuesday 27: Britain announces that it is willing to resume the Lausanne peace talks with Turkey.

Wednesday 28: The Italian Royal Air Force is founded.

Thursday 29: Thousands line the streets of Paris to watch the funeral procession of the actress Sarah Bernhardt, who died on 27 March.

March 1923

An obsessive fan, Marina Vega, breaks into Charlie Chaplin's home in Hollywood. After explaining she travelled from Mexico City, Chaplin gets her to leave by promising to buy her a train ticket home.

Friday 30: Lieutenants Batelier and Carrier set a new air record of flying 500 km (310.7 miles) in 2 hours 42 minutes, an average of 184 kph (114 mph) at Etampee, France.

Saturday 31: Eleven people are killed when French troops fire on passively-resisting demonstrators in Essen, occupied Germany.

America's first dance marathon ends at the Audabon Ballroom, New York City. Alma Cummings completes 27 hours of non-stop dancing with six male partners.

April 1923

Sunday 1: The comedy film *Safety Last* starring Harold Lloyd is released.

The provisional Government of Ireland sets up customs posts on the land border with British-controlled Northern Ireland.

Monday 2: The Soviet Union officially rejects complaints by the Polish government over the execution of a Polish Roman Catholic priest, Father Konstantin Budkevich, for alleged anti-communist activities.

Harold Lloyd in a scene from the film *Safety Last*, released on 1 April.

April 1923

Above: on 3 April, 'Curley' becomes the first officially recognised survivor of Custer's Last Stand of 1876.

Tuesday 3: The controversy over whether anybody survived the 1876 Battle of the Little Big Horn, also known as 'Custer's Last Stand' is settled when the claim of an alleged survivor, an Indian scout named Curley, is officially recognised by the US Department of the Interior.

Wednesday 4: The Warner Brothers film studio is founded.

Actor Peter Vaughan (Grouty in *Porridge*) is born in Wem, Shropshire (died 2016).

The mathematician John Venn, inventor of the Venn Diagram, dies aged 88.

Thursday 5: Lord Carnarvon, discoverer of the tomb of Tutankhamun in Egypt, dies aged 56, fuelling speculation in the press over 'King Tut's Curse'.

Friday 6: The jazz trumpeter Louis Armstrong makes his recording debut, playing *Chimes Blues* with King Oliver's Creole Band.

Saturday 7: Nine IRA members die in a shoot-out with Irish government forces in Glencar, County Kerry.

Mrs Lillie Groom wins the London to Brighton Baby Carriage race, pushing her pram (with baby) the 52 miles in 12 hours 20 minutes.

The world ballroom dancing record is set by Ruth Holleck and Jack Butler who dance for 36 h 13 m in New York.

Louis Armstrong records his first song on 6 April.

Sunday 8: Princess Yolanda, eldest daughter of Italy's King Victor Emmanuel and Queen Helena, is married to Count Calvi di Bergolo in Rome.

A dance marathon in the USA.

Monday 9: Harvard University passes a motion banning discrimination on grounds of race.

Tuesday 10: A ban on the new craze of ballroom dancing marathons is put into effect in Sunderland, England, where the first world record dance was set on 18 February.

Wednesday 11: In the Irish Civil War, six Republican combatants known as the 'Tuam Martyrs' are executed by provisional Irish government forces in Tuam, County Galway.

Thursday 12: Phonofilm, the first workable talking picture system, is demonstrated by its inventor Lee de Forest in New York City. The first talking picture (using a different system) is released in 1927.

Sean O' Casey's play *The Shadow of a Gunman* opens in Dublin.

Friday 13: Russia suffers from unlucky Friday the Thirteenth as floods hit Moscow and an earthquake strikes Kamchatka, killing 36.

Saturday 14: A ballroom dancing marathon in Baltimore, Maryland, is stopped by police after 53 hours.

Singer Eddie Cantor is the first big star to be filmed in Phonofilm, the talking-picture process first demonstrated on 12 April.

April 1923

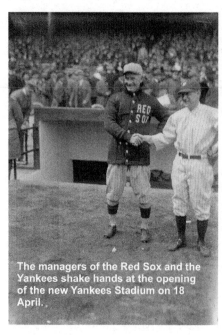

The managers of the Red Sox and the Yankees shake hands at the opening of the new Yankees Stadium on 18 April.

Sunday 15: Insulin goes on the market in the USA.

Monday 16: Britain's Conservative government issues its Budget, with cuts to income tax and alcohol duty.

The 27th Boston Marathon is won by Clarence DeMar for the second time, in 2.23.37.

Tuesday 17: In the Irish Civil War, the anti-Treaty politician Daniel Breen is arrested by the provisional Irish government.

The film director Lindsay Anderson (*If*) is born in Bangalore, India (died 1994).

Wednesday 18: 74,200 attend the opening baseball game at the Yankees Stadium in New York City; Babe Ruth hits the venue's first home run.

Thursday 19: Five people are killed during clashes with occupying French troops in Mulheim, Germany.

Friday 20: The German Nazi Party's newspaper, *Die Stürmer,* is published for the first time.

The Latin band leader Tito Puente is born in New York City (died 2000).

Saturday 21: The first production of a Shakespeare play in modern dress, *Cymbeline*, opens at the Birmingham Repertory Theatre.

Barry Jackson, director of the first Shakespeare play performed in modern dress on 21 April.

Sunday 22: The TV producer Aaron Spelling (*Charlie's Angels*) is born in Dallas, Texas (died 2006).

Monday 23: Cannabis is banned in Canada.

Princess Louise of Prussia, daughter of Kaiser Wilhelm I, dies aged 84.

Tuesday 24: Benito Mussolini forms a military reserve force of 500,000 men from disparate Fascist groups.

Wednesday 25: The blues guitarist Albert King (*Born Under A Bad Sign*) is born in Indianola, Mississippi (died 1992).

Thursday 26: The wedding of the Duke of York (the future King George VI) and Lady Elizabeth Bowes-Lyon (the future Queen Elizabeth, the Queen Mother) takes place in Westminster Abbey.

Friday 27: The Irish nationalist leader Eamon de Valera announces he is willing to agree to a ceasefire in the Irish Civil War.

The Royal Wedding of 26 April (l-r): The Earl and Countess of Strathmore; the Duke and Duchess of York (later King George VI and Queen Elizabeth the Queen Mother), Queen Mary and King George V.

April 1923

Left: A policeman on a white horse holds back the crowd at the FA Cup Final on 28 April.

Saturday 28: The legendary 'White Horse Cup Final' takes place at the newly opened Wembley Stadium in London where Bolton Wanderers beat West Ham 2-0. A lone police constable, PC George Scorey, mounted on a white horse named Billie, enables the football game to go ahead by holding back a crowd of thousands of fans who attempt to invade the pitch.

Sunday 29: The French government announces it will send 20,000 troops into Syria to protect its League of Nations mandate against Turkish forces massing on the border.

Monday 30: The US Supreme Court allows US ships to sell alcohol three miles offshore. Alcohol sales are banned elsewhere due to Prohibition.

May
1923

Tuesday 1: Large-scale May Day socialist gatherings take place across Britain, with trade unions condemning the French occupation of Germany's Ruhr region.

Wednesday 2: The newly formed British Broadcasting Company (BBC) moves to Savoy Hill House in the Strand, London.

Thursday 3: Oakley Kelly and John Mcready complete the first US transcontinental crossing by air, flying from New York to San Diego in 26 hours 50 minutes.

Friday 4: Canada bans Chinese immigration.

The comedian Eric Sykes is born in Oldham, Lancashire (died 2012).

Left: pilots Kelly and Mcready shake hands after making the first crossing of the USA by air on 3 May.

May 1923

Left: Jess Willard is the first boxer to win a match at the new Yankees Stadium on 12 May.

Saturday 5: Radio broadcasting begins in Singapore.

Sunday 6: 150 passengers including two American and an Englishman are taken hostage when bandits seize a train near Nanjing, China.

Monday 7: The kings of Sweden, Norway and Denmark meet in Copenhagen for their seven-year talks on Scandinavian governance.

Tuesday 8: Briton Joseph Rothman and an unidentified American are shot dead during a gun battle between Chinese bandits and troops on a train near Nanjing.

Wednesday 9: The Chinese government agrees to pay the hostage demanded by the bandits holding a train to ransom near Nanjing.

Thursday 10: Vatslav Vorosky, Soviet delegate to the Lausanne conference on Turkish borders, is assassinated by a Swiss army officer.

Friday 11: Ten home runs are scored during a baseball game between the St Louis Cardinals and Philadelphia Phillies. The record holds until 1966.

Amelia Earhart qualifies as a pilot on 15 May.

Saturday 12: The first boxing match takes place in the new Yankees stadium; a crowd of 63,000 watches Jess Willard knock out Floyd Johnson.

Sunday 13: French Prime Minister Raymond Poincare announces that French troops will remain in Germany's Ruhr district until war reparations are paid.

Monday 14: Italian fascist leader Benito Mussolini addresses the International Women's Suffrage Congress in Rome, expressing his support for votes for women.

Tuesday 15: The aviatrix Amelia Earhart receives her pilot's licence.

The British protectorate of Transjordan is granted semi-autonomous status under King Abdullah I.

Wednesday 16: Following an attack by government troops, the Chinese bandits who took 150 train passengers hostage move their remaining captives to a stronghold near Paotzuku.

Thursday 17: The actress and singer Marlene Dietrich marries director Rudolf Sieber in Berlin.

Friday 18: Two members of the Michigan based House of David sect are jailed during a long-running investigation into misconduct by the group, followers of the 19th century English prophetess Joanna Southcott.

Mussolini announces his support for women's suffrage on 14 May.

May 1923

Comedian Larry Semon begins a $1m per year contract on 22 May.

Saturday 19: The British Prime Minister, Andrew Bonar Law returns prematurely to London from a Paris trip amid rumours that he is seriously ill.

Sunday 20: Prime Minister Bonar Law announces his retirement following a cancer diagnosis.

Monday 21: The comedy play *Aren't We All?* By Frederick Lonsdale and starring Leslie Howard opens on Broadway.

British Prime Minister Bonar Law undergoes an operation for cancer of the throat; no successor has yet been appointed.

Tuesday 22: The comedian Larry Semon becomes one of Hollywood's highest paid stars when he begins a $1m per year contract with Tru-Art Film Corporation of New York.

Wednesday 23: The Belgian national airline SABENA *(Societé Anonyme Belge d'Exploitation de la Navigation Aérienne)* is founded.

Stanley Baldwin replaces Andrew Bonar as Britain's Prime Minister.

Thursday 24: The Irish Civil War effectively ends after the nationalist leader Eamon de Valera orders the Irish Rebublican Army to surrender.

Friday 25: 2200 die when a 5.7 magnitude earthquake hits the Razavi province of Iran.

Stanley Baldwin becomes British Prime Minister on 23 May.

The start of the first Le Mans motor race, 27 May.

Saturday 26: Seven people are killed as strikes and demonstrations against French occupation spread in the Ruhr region of Germany.

Sunday 27: The first '24 Hours of Le Mans' motor endurance race is won by André Lagache and René Léonard of France.

Left: French troops occupy Essen, Germany: seven people are killed in anti-French rioting in the region on 26 May.

Monday 28: The city of San Francisco lifts a ban on persons dressing as the opposite sex, allowing the practice unless done 'with intent to deceive.'

Tuesday 29: The French aviator Georges Barbot becomes the first pilot to cross the English Channel in a powered glider; he

May 1923

Left: Tommy Milton, winner of the 1923 Indianapolis 500 motor race on 30 May.

Prince Rainier of Monaco is born on 31 May.

uses his tiny 15 hp engine only for the ascent, and the crossing costs 6d (2.5 new pence) in petrol.

Wednesday 30: Half a million striking German miners agree to return to work after the government offers a 50% pay rise.

Tommy Milton wins the Indianapolis 500 motor race.

Thursday 31: Prince Rainier III of Monaco is born (died 2005).

June
1923

Friday 1: Ten people are killed in a protest in Mexico City against government restrictions on church affairs.

Saturday 2: New York City announces the electrification of all its railway lines by 1926.

Eugene Criqui of France beats Johnny Kilbane of the USA to win the World Featherweight Boxing title.

Sunday 3: A temperance referendum in Switzerland rejects a proposed ban on home distilling of spirits.

Turkish delegates to the Lausanne Conference; the talks break down on 5 June.

June 1923

Edgar Wallace becomes the first BBC radio sports commentator on 6 June.

The family of the late Lord Carnarvon announces his collection of artefacts, including the treasure of Tutankhamun, will be presented to the British Museum.

Monday 4: The French aviator George Barbot who crossed the English Channel in his 'flying flivver' micro-plane on 29 May, is forced to abandon his first US flight due to bad weather. Barbot claims a transatlantic flight can be made in his plane with just $50 worth of fuel.

Tuesday 5: The Lausanne Conference on the future of Turkey's borders reaches a stalemate.

Wednesday 6: Papyrus wins the Epsom Derby.

The mystery writer Edgar Wallace becomes the first sports commentator on BBC radio when he reports on the event.

Thursday 7: The Federation of British Industries is granted a Royal Charter.

The ballroom dancing marathon record is set at 147 hours by Miss Hilda Johnson of St Louis, Missouri.

Friday 8: France rejects new war reparations proposals from Germany; the French Prime Minister Raymond Poincaré refuses to discuss the matter while there is still unrest in the occupied Ruhr region of Germany.

Above: French PM Poincaré rejects German proposals on 8 June.

Above: poster for the film *The Shock*, released on 10 June.

Saturday 9: Aleksander Tsankov seizes control of Bulgaria in a bloodless coup.

Princess Helena, third daughter of Queen Victoria, dies aged 77.

Sunday 10: The drama film *The Shock* starring Lon Chaney is released.

The newspaper magnate and fraudster Robert Maxwell MC (Ján Ludvík Hyman Binyamin Hoch) is born in Slatinské Doly, Czechoslovakia (died 1991).

Monday 11: The Chinese train hostage crisis, which began on 6 May, ends as the final eight passengers are released by bandits.

Tuesday 12: A volunteer force of 100,000 men loyal to King Boris of Bulgaria is formed to oppose the country's recent coup.

Wednesday 13: Li Yuanhong, President of China, is arrested by government troops as warlords attempt to force his resignation.

Thursday 14: Gao Lingwei becomes acting President of China.

Friday 15: Arthur Havers wins the British Open golf tournament.

Lou Gehrig makes his baseball debut for the New York Yankees.

Saturday 16: French troops seize Dortmund railway station, leaving only one

Aleksander Tsankov seizes control of Bulgaria in a coup on 9 June.

rail route out of occupied Germany.

Sunday 17: Mount Etna in Sicily erupts.

Monday 18: The US black political leader Marcus Garvey is found guilty of mail fraud.

The industrialist Henry Ford denies rumours that he is standing for the US Presidency.

Tuesday 19: Britain and the USA reach an agreement on the settlement of British war debts.

Arthur Havers wins the British Open golf tournament on 15 June.

Wednesday 20: US President Warren G Harding begins a national speaking tour entitled 'The Voyage of Understanding.'

Thursday 21: US President Warren G Harding becomes the first President to be heard by a million people at once, as he makes a speech broadcast by three radio stations.

Friday 22: The British Parliament passes the Oxford and Cambridge Universities Act 1923 resulting in greater funding for both establishments.

Revealing bathing costumes such as these shown above are banned in Atlantic City on 23 June.

Saturday 23: Ladies' bathing suits revealing more length of leg above the knee than below are

The black separatist leader Marcus Garvey is convicted of fraud on 18 June.

banned from the beach at Atlantic City, New Jersey.

Sunday 24: Britain's former Prime Minister David Lloyd George states in an address to the London Welsh Baptist Chapel that Prohibition in the USA is a 'bold experiment' which should be 'given a fair chance'.

Monday 25: Howard Ferguson becomes Premier of Ontario.

Tuesday 26: Britain's Prime Minister Stanley Baldwin announces that the Royal Air Force will be increased from 18 to 52 squadrons.

Wednesday 27: A fire causes major damage in China's Forbidden City.

Four Labour MPs are suspended from Britain's parliament when they refuse to come to order in a debate over health care.

Thursday 28: Mustafa Kemal Ataturk is victorious in Turkey's general election. His party is the only one standing for office.

Friday 29: France's Prime Minister Raymond Poincaré emphatically denies suggestions that his country wishes to annexe the Ruhr region of Germany, stating that the military occupation is only until Germany pays her war debts.

Saturday 30: As protests grow over the Franco-Belgian occupation, a bomb explodes on a train in the Ruhr region of Germany, killing ten Belgian soldiers.

Right: Mustafa Kemal Ataturk is victorious in Turkey on 28 June.

July
1923

Henry Seagrave wins the French Grand Prix on 2 July.

Sunday 1: France announces the building of four new submarines.

Monday 2: Britain's Henry Seagrave wins the French Grand Prix motor race.

Tuesday 3: Four Germans are shot dead by French troops in the occupied Rhineland region of Germany, for breaking a curfew.

Wednesday 4: Jack Dempsey beats Tommy Gibbons to retain the World Heavyweight boxing championship title.

Thursday 5: The actress Ethel Barrymore is divorced from husband Russell G Colt.

Friday 6: Suzanne Lenglen wins the womens' tennis finals at Wimbledon.

Saturday 7: Bill Johnston wins the mens' tennis finals at Wimbledon.

Sunday 8: Warren G Harding becomes the first US President to visit Alaska.

Monday 9: Pilot Russell Maughan is unsuccessful in the first attempt to cross the continental US by air in one solar day. The feat is not achieved until 1924.

Tuesday 10: The actor and music-hall comedian Albert Chevalier dies aged 62.

Suzanne Lenglen wins Wimbledon on 6 July.

Wednesday 11: The French government announces it will not engage in further conferences to discuss German war reparations, claiming the matter was fully and finally settled with the 1919 Treaty of Versailles.

Thursday 12: Britain's Prime Minister Stanley Baldwin states that Germany cannot be forced to pay her war debts as this will result in 'economic chaos.'

Friday 13: The 'Hollywoodland' sign is erected above Hollywood, California. Originally used to advertise a housing estate, the sign is shortened to the better known name of 'Hollywood' in the 1940s.

The Hollywood sign is erected on 13 July.

July 1923

The Mexican revolutionary leader Pancho Villa is assassinated on 20 July.

Saturday 14: Hermann Erhardt, leader of the Kapp Putsch of 1920 which attempted to restore the rule of Kaiser Wilhelm, escapes from prison before his treason trial begins.

Sunday 15: The 656 mile Alaska Railroad is completed.

Monday 16: The first Ku Kux Klan meeting to admit female members is held in Asheville, North Carolina.

Italy and Britain agree to a conference on German war reparations without France's involvement.

Tuesday 17: The leaders of Northern Ireland and the newly formed Irish Free State meet in London for talks on border controls.

Wednesday 18: Winston Churchill appears in court in a case brought by Lord Alfred Douglas alleging Churchill lied about the progress of the First World War for financial gain. The case is dismissed and Douglas is imprisoned.

The Alaska Railroad under construction. The 656-mile-long road is completed on 15 July.

July 1923

Ramsay MacDonald, leader of HM Opposition, calls for an arms treaty on 23 July.

England's Matrimonial Causes Act is passed, allowing women to divorce men for adultery.

Thursday 19: The pilot Russell Maughan makes his second attempt to fly across the continental USA in one solar day; he again ends in failure as technical problems force him to land in Wyoming.

Friday 20: The Mexican revolutionary Pancho Villa is assassinated.

Saturday 21: Six people are killed in rioting in Breslau, Germany, over the sudden rise in food prices caused by hyperinflation.

Sunday 22: Henri Pélissier wins the Tour de France.

Monday 23: Britain's parliament rejects proposals by the Leader of the Opposition, Ramsay MacDonald, for an international conference on arms limitation.

Tuesday 24: The Lausanne Treaty is signed. It is the final treaty of the First World War, which sets out peace terms between the western Allies and Turkey.

Wednesday 25: The actress Estelle Getty (*The Golden Girls*) is born in New York City (died 2008).

Thursday 26: Warren G Harding becomes the first US President to visit Canada.

Henri Pélissier wins the Tour de France on 22 July.

July 1923

Jazz legend Sidney Bechet (shown here in 1954) makes his first record on 30 July.

Friday 27: US President Warren G Harding gives his last speech.

Saturday 28: Work begins on Australia's Sydney Harbour Bridge.

Sunday 29: Four people are killed when fighting breaks out between communists and police in Brandenburg, Germany.

Monday 30: The jazz clarinetist Sidney Bechet makes his recording debut on *Wild Cat Blues.*

Tuesday 31: The minimum age for drinking alcohol in British public houses is raised from 14 to 18.

August
1923

Wednesday 1: US President Warren G Harding is reported to be gravely ill.

Thursday 2: US President Warren G Harding dies from heart failure aged 57.

The future Israeli President and Prime Minister Shimon Peres is born in Wiszniew, Poland (died 2016).

Friday 3: Calvin Coolidge is inaugurated as President of the USA in the early hours of the morning; he is sworn in by his father, a public notary.

Far left: President Harding dies on 2 August and is replaced by Vice-President Calvin Coolidge.

August 1923

Warren G Harding's body lies in state at the White House; a ten day period of official mourning is declared on 4 August.

Saturday 4: US President Calvin Coolidge declares a ten day period of mourning for his recently deceased predecessor, Warren G Harding.

Sunday 5: French occupying forces in the Ruhr region of Germany impose an 11pm curfew following a bomb attack on a military band.

Monday 6: Henry Sullivan becomes the first American to swim the English Channel, with a time of 27 hours 25 minutes.

Tuesday 7: Germany's Chancellor Wilhelm Cuno announces the Mark will be put back on the gold standard.

Wednesday 8: US President Warren G Harding's state funeral is held in the Capitol Rotunda, Washington, DC.

Thursday 9: A wave of strikes takes place across Germany in protest at hyperinflation.

Left: Henry Sullivan becomes the first American to swim the English Channel on 6 August.

The historic Washington Elm is declared dead on 13 August.

Friday 10: The German President bans the publication or distribution of any material calling for the overthrow of the government.

Saturday 11: 35 people are killed as protests against the German government spread nationwide.

Sunday 12: Wilhelm Cuno resigns as Chancellor of Germany following further rioting in which 30 people are killed.

Enrique Tirabocci of Argentina swims the English Channel in a record 16 hours 33 minutes.

Monday 13: The ancient tree known as the Washington Elm in Cambridge, Massachussets, under which General Washington supposedly took command of the American army in 1775, is declared dead.

Gustav Stressman becomes Chancellor of Germany.

Tuesday 14: 99 miners are killed in a pit explosion in Kemmerer, Wyoming.

Wednesday 15: The Irish nationalist leader Eamon de Valera is arrested by Free State authorities while making a speech in Ennis, County Clare.

Gustav Stressman becomes Chancellor of Germany on 13 August.

August 1923

Above: singer Jim Reeves is born on 20 August. Below: entertainer Larry Grayson is born on 21 August.

Thursday 16: Thousands are bankrupted when the Home Bank of Canada collapses.

Friday 17: As relations between the USA and Japan worsen, Britain revokes the Anglo-Japanese Treaty, signed during the Russo-Japanese war of 1904.

Saturday 18: The first national track and field events for women are held in Britain at the Oxo Sports Ground, London.

Sunday 19: At least 200 people are killed when a hurricane hits the Portuguese colony of Macau near Hong Kong.

Monday 20: Tram fares rise by 1000% in two weeks as hyperinflation worsens in Germany.

The country singer Jim Reeves is born in Galloway, Texas (died 1964).

Tuesday 21: The TV presenter Larry Grayson is born in Banbury, Oxfordshire (died 1995).

Wednesday 22: Spain sends 5000 more troops to Morocco in the Rif War against Berber tribes.

Thursday 23: Kato Tomasaburo, Prime Minister of Japan, dies suddenly aged 62.

Allied forces begin their withdrawal from Constantinople following the signing of the Lausanne Treaty with Turkey.

Friday 24: The speed record for the US transcontinental air mail is set at 26 hours 14 minutes.

Above: Lon Chaney as Quasimodo and Patsy Ruth Miller as Esmerelda in a scene from *The Hunchback of Notre Dame*, released on 30 August.

Saturday 25: Laying of the sixth and largest transatlantic telegraph cable begins at Far Rockaway, New York.

Maine Road stadium, home of Manchester City Football Club until 2003, opens.

Sunday 26: The French government rejects a German offer to partially pay its war reparations by granting a share of its industries to France.

Monday 27: The Bulgarian ambassador to Czechoslovakia, Rayko Daskaloff, is assassinated.

Neville Chamberlain takes over from Stanley Baldwin as Britain's Chancellor of the Exchequer.

Tuesday 28: The US Army pilots Lowell Smith and John Richter stay in flight for a record 37 hours, circling over San Diego and using mid-air refueling.

Wednesday 29: The director and actor Sir Richard Attenborough is born in Cambridge (died 2014).

Thursday 30: The film *The Hunchback of Notre Dame* starring Lon Chaney is released.

Friday 31: Italian forces occupy the Greek island of Corfu in retaliation for the murder of an Italian general in Greece.

September 1923

Saturday 1: 120,000 people are killed when a devastating earthquake destroys most of Tokyo, Japan.

The boxer Rocky Marciano is born in Brockton, Mass. (died 1969).

Noel Coward: his musical *London Calling* opens on 4 September.

Sunday 2: The Greek government calls for an international enquiry into the 'Corfu Incident' involving the death of an Italian general.

Monday 3: The historical drama film *Rosita* starring Mary Pickford is released.

Tuesday 4: Italian leader Benito Mussolini threatens to withdraw his country from the League of Nations if it becomes involved in his occupation of Corfu.

The Noel Coward musical *London Calling* opens at London's Duke of York's theatre.

Wednesday 5: The campaign of strikes against French occupation of the Ruhr region of Germany largely comes to an

The boxer Rocky Marciano is born on 1 September.
on 28 August.

end as coal miners return to work.

The Jerome Kern musical comedy *The Beauty Prize* opens at the Winter Garden Theatre, London.

Thursday 6: King Peter II of Yugoslavia is born in Belgrade (died 1970).

Friday 7: Mary Katherine Campbell becomes the only beauty queen to win the Miss America contest three years running.

Saturday 8: The Honda Point disaster, the deadliest peacetime incident in US Navy history takes place. 23 sailors die off the coast when seven ships run aground off the Californian coast.

Sunday 9: Carlo Salamano wins the Italian Grand Prix motor race.

Monday 10: The newly formed Irish Free State (now the Republic of Ireland) joins the League of Nations.

A total solar eclipse takes place across much of the Pacific Ocean and southern California.

Tuesday 11: Six die as unemployed Germans riot in Dresden in protest over hyperinflation.

Wednesday 12: Southern Rhodesia becomes a British crown colony.

Thursday 13: General Miguel Primo de Rivera seizes control of Spain in a military coup.

General Primo de Rivera takes over Spain on 13 September.

September 1923

Gloria Swanson stars in the drama film *Zaza*, released on 16 September.

Friday 14: Jack Dempsey retains his World Heavyweight boxing title when he knocks out the contender Luis Angel Firpo at the Polo Grounds, New York City.

Saturday 15: Martial law is declared in the US state of Oklahoma following fighting between the Ku Kux Klan and opposition groups.

Sunday 16: The romantic film *Zaza*, starring Gloria Swanson is released.

The Harold Lloyd comedy film, *Why Worry?* is released.

Monday 17: The play *Outward Bound* by Sutton Vane, about a group of passengers on a mysterious ocean liner, is first performed.

584 homes are destroyed when a major fire spreads across the town of Berkeley, California.

Tuesday 18: Queen Anne of Romania is born in Paris, France (died 2016).

Only one combined newspaper is published in New York City due to a press strike.

Wednesday 19: Germany concedes to France's demands for war reparations and agrees to end the civil disobedience campaign against French occupation of the Ruhr region.

Thursday 20: A communist-led coup takes place in Bulgaria.

The writer Jimmy Perry, co-creator of the BBC comedy series *Dad's Army*, is born in Barnes, Surrey (died 2016).

Queen Anne the Queen Consort of Romania is born on 18 September.

September 1923

Friday 21: The three day New York press strike ends.

Saturday 22: 600 people are arrested in Chicago in a major clampdown on speakeasies (illegal drinking clubs).

The poet Dannie Abse is born in Cardiff (died 2014).

Sunday 23: King Boris III of Bulgaria declares a state of emergency following the recent coup.

Monday 24: The Governor of Oklahoma orders all armed citizens to come to the protection of the state as violence continues between the Ku Kuk Klan and rival groups.

Above: the first issue of _Radio Times_ is published on 28 September.

Tuesday 25: The German government officially ends its policy of passive resistance to French and Belgian occupying forces.

Wednesday 26: The film _A Woman of Paris_, directed by Charlie Chaplin, is released.

Bulgarian troops loyal to the King are mobilised against the new government who have siezed power following a recent coup.

Thursday 27: Occupying Italian forces withdraw from Corfu following a meeting of the Allied powers to end the Corfu Crisis.

Bulgarian forces capture the city of Ferdinand from rebel troops, ending the recent uprising.

Friday 28: The first issue of the BBC listings magazine _Radio Times_ is published.

Saturday 29: Palestine comes under British rule.

September 1923

Sunday 30: 16 people are killed in rioting in Dusseldorf, Germany by Rhenish Republic separatists; on the same day an attempted coup against the German government takes place Berlin.

The French airship *Dixmude* makes a record non-stop flight of 118 hours from Paris to the Sahara and back again.

The pianist and composer Donald Swann of Flanders and Swann is born in Llanelli, Carmarthenshire (died 1994).

Left: poster for the Charlie Chaplin film *A Woman of Paris*, released on 26 September.

Above: Palestine comes under British rule on 29 September following the collapse of the Ottoman Empire. Here, the new High Commissioner, Viscount Samuel (in car, right) meets Arab residents.

October 1923

Monday 1: The 1923 Imperial Conference meets in London to decide on the foreign policies of the British Dominions.

The French boxer Georges Carpentier knocks out Britain's Joe Beckett to win the World Heavyweight Championship title.

Tuesday 2: An attempted coup in Germany (the Kustrin Putsch) is put down by government troops.

Wednesday 3: The entire German cabinet resigns over plans by the Chancellor to invoke sweeping powers to combat the country's economic crisis.

Thursday 4: The actor Charlton Heston is born in Cook County, Illinois (died 2008).

Five men are rescued from a flooded mine in Falkirk, Stirlingshire, after being trapped for ten days.

Friday 5: Cao Kun becomes President of China.

Saturday 6: Czech Airlines is founded.

Left: Georges Carpentier becomes the World Heavyweight boxing champion on 1 October.

October 1923

A new German cabinet is formed following the mass resignation of 3 October; it consists of exactly the same men with just one substitution.

Sunday 7: The former British Prime Minister David Lloyd George begins a tour of Canada.

Monday 8: The musical comedy play *Battling Butler*, later made into a film starring Buster Keaton, opens on Broadway.

Tuesday 9: As the German economic situation worsens, the state governor of Bavaria introduces the death penalty for food profiteering.

Wednesday 10: The US Navy's first rigid airship, the USS *Shenandoah*, is commissioned.

The sports commentator Murray Walker is born in Birmingham (died 2021).

Thursday 11: 26 die when the SS *City of Everett* sinks in the Gulf of Mexico.

The USS *Shenandoah* is commissioned on 10 October.

Friday 12: Food riots break out in Dusseldorf, Germany.

Saturday 13: The capital of Turkey is moved from Istanbul to Ankara.

Sunday 14: A bomb explodes at the Wrigley Field baseball ground in Chicago, causing major damage; no culprit is found but trade union agitators are suspected.

Monday 15: The German government announces plans for the new Rentenmark currency to replace the hyperinflated Mark.

The baseball World Series is won by the New York Yankees who defeat the New York Giants 4-2.

Above: Julius the Cat, the cartoon star of the new Disney studios which open on 16 October.

Tuesday 16: The Walt Disney company is founded, as the Disney Brothers Studio begins work on a series of cartoons starring Julius the Cat.

Wednesday 17: As social unrest continues, the German states of Saxony and Thuringia are put under martial law.

Thursday 18: Britain's Ministry of Transport urges local councils to take action against the spread of unsightly advertising billboards alongside roads.

Friday 19: The US Prohibition commissioner announces a clampdown on 'the menacing traffic in home brew ingredients.'

Saturday 20: All foreigners are ordered to leave Changshaw province in China as fighting intensifies between local warlords.

Sunday 21: The separatist Rhenish Republic (allied with France) is declared in western Germany.

October 1923

Robin Day is born on 24 October.

Monday 22: A communist uprising takes place in Hamburg, Germany.

Tuesday 23: Occupying Belgian troops impose martial law in the area of the newly declared Rhenish Republic in Germany, as fighting between rival political factions breaks out.

Wednesday 24: Communist leaders in Germany decide against pushing for a nationwide revolution; fighting continues in Hamburg.

The BBC broadcaster Sir Robin Day is born in Oxford (died 2000).

Thursday 25: The communist uprising in Hamburg, Germany, ends; hundreds of party members are arrested.

Friday 26: Great Britain, France and the USA agree to set up a reparations commission for Allied war debts.

Saturday 27: 23 people are killed during political protests in Freiburg, Germany.

Right: a young couple demonstrate the Charleston dance: the craze begins on 29 October.

Above, left: former Prime Minister Bonar Law dies on 30 October.
Right: Reza Khan becomes Prime Minister of Iran on 28 October.

The 'pop art' artist Roy Lichtenstein is born in New York City (died 1997).

Sunday 28: Reza Khan becomes Prime Minister of Iran.

Monday 29: The Republic of Turkey is proclaimed.

Martial law is imposed in Dresden, Germany.

The Broadway musical *Runnin' Wild* opens; one of its numbers, 'Charleston' launches a new dance craze.

Tuesday 30: The former British Prime Minister Andrew Bonar Law dies after a short illness, aged 65.

Wednesday 31: Riots and looting break out in Melbourne, Australia following a police strike.

November 1923

Thursday 1: The Finnish national airline Finnair is founded.

Friday 2: As inflation reaches its peak in Germany, the Reichsbank issues a 100 trillion Reichsmark note.

Saturday 3: Louise Mountbatten, sister of Lord Mountbatten of Burma, marries Crown Prince (later King) Gustav Adolf of Sweden at St James' Palace, London.

Sunday 4: Adolf Hitler prepares a coup in Germany during a military parade in Munich, but calls it off at the last minute due to a large police presence.

Monday 5: Unemployed rioters loot shops in Berlin, Germany, and attack Jews, whom they blame for high food prices.

Tuesday 6: A failed Communist uprising takes place in Poland.

Left: Louise Mountbatten becomes Crown Princess of Sweden on 3 November.

Left: Adolf Hitler with the leaders of the attempted coup in Germany on 9 November.

Wednesday 7: The Imperial Conference in London approves a protectionist tariff plan for goods from the British Empire.

Thursday 8: Adolf Hitler is brought to the attention of the world when he leads 2000 Nazi Party members in an attempted coup (the 'Beer Hall Putsch') in Munich.

Friday 9: 16 Nazis are killed in clashes with the police in Munich as the Beer Hall Putsch is suppressed; the Nazi Party is banned in Germany.

Saturday 10: Crown Prince Wilhelm of Germany returns home from exile in Holland. His father, Kaiser Wilhelm II, remains in exile until his death in 1941.

The big-band singer Anne Shelton is born in London (died 1994).

Crown Prince Wilhelm, the Kaiser's son, returns to Germany from exile on 10 November.

Sunday 11: Following the attempted coup of 8 November, Nazi leader Adolf Hitler is arrested after being found hiding in an attic.

Monday 12: The flag of the Soviet Union,

November 1923

Germany's new currency, the *Rentenmark*, is launched on 20 November. It is backed by land revenues rather than gold.

a hammer and sickle on a red background, is flown for the first time.

Tuesday 13: France makes a formal protest over the return of Germany's Crown Prince Wilhelm from exile, claiming it breaches the Treaty of Versailles.

Wednesday 14: Germany suspends war reparations payments; all cafes in Berlin are ordered to allow the unemployed and homeless to shelter in them.

Thursday 15: Germany's hyperinflation peaks at 4.2 trillion Marks to one US dollar.

Friday 16: Britain's Prime Minister Stanley Baldwin dissolves Parliament as he calls for a snap general election over new imperial trade tariffs.

Italy's leader Benito Mussolini formally condemns the French and Belgian occupation of parts of Germany.

Saturday 17: 24 people die in food riots in the Ruhr region of Germany.

Sunday 18: The first American astronaut, Alan Shepard, is born in Derry, New Hampshire (died 1998).

Left: Astronaut Alan Shepard is born on 18 November.

A young acting newcomer, Humphrey Bogart, makes one of his early stage appearances on 26 November.

Monday 19: Britain's Prime Minister Stanley Baldwin calls for protective tariffs to aid British industry, stating 'we must keep the home fires burning.'

Tuesday 20: The new German Rentenmark is launched, tied to land revenues, ending the country's hyperinflation problem.

Wednesday 21: Frank Goddard beats Jack Bloomfield at the Royal Albert Hall, London, to reclaim the British heavyweight boxing title.

Thursday 22: British archaeologist Robert MacAlister confirms the discovery of traces of the biblical City of David near Jerusalem.

Friday 23: Gustav Stresemann resigns as Chancellor of Germany following a vote of no confidence.

Saturday 24: In an early example of the life-saving power of radio, a sailor dying of acute gastritis on the SS *Venetian* is successfully treated according to instructions sent over the radio by a doctor 1200 miles away in California.

Sunday 25: The British vessel *Tomoka* is intercepted by US Customs attempting to land 200 cases of rum off the coast of New Jersey. It is the last major seizure before Prohibition rules are extended to twelve miles offshore.

Lionel Barrymore stars in the play *Laugh Clown, Laugh,* which opens on 28 November.

November 1923

Marlene Dietrich, shown here in 1930, makes her first screen appearance on 29 November.

Monday 26: The comedy play *Meet the Wife* opens on Broadway, its cast includes the 24 year old Humphrey Bogart in one of his first acting roles.

Tuesday 27: The first radio contact with the North Pole is made, as the Macmillan polar expedition exchanges messages with army signallers in Hartford, Connecticut.

Wednesday 28: The musical comedy *Laugh Clown, Laugh*, opens on Broadway starring Lionel Barrymore and Irene Fenwick.

Thursday 29: Marlene Dietrich makes her film debut in the Germany comedy *The Little Napoleon.*

Friday 30: Wilhelm Marx becomes Chancellor of Germany.

Wilhelm Marx becomes Chancellor of Germany on 30 November.

December
1923

The epic film *The Ten Commandments* is first shown on 4 December.

Saturday 1: 356 die when the Gleno Dam bursts in Bergamo, Italy.

The Irish Free State government begins the release of captured 'diehard' fighters (those opposed to the Free State compromise with Britain).

Sunday 2: The opera singer Maria Callas is born in New York City (died 1977).

Monday 3: The Joseph Conrad novel *The Rover* is published.

Tuesday 4: The epic film *The Ten Commandments* directed by Cecil B De Mille, premieres in Hollywood.

Wednesday 5: Major flooding takes place in northern Italy as the Toce Dam bursts.

Thursday 6: Britain's first Labour government is formed after the

December 1923

WB Yeats receives the Nobel Prize for Literature on 10 December.

Conservatives are defeated in the general election.

Friday 7: Further large earthquakes hit Japan, although there is no loss of life.

Saturday 8: Germany's new Chancellor Wilhelm Marx is granted sweeping powers to cope with the country's economic crisis.

Sunday 9: Nine people are killed in a train crash near Forsythe, New York.

Monday 10: The poet William Butler Yeats wins the Nobel Prize for Literature.

Tuesday 11: The Mexican government announces it is in 'complete control' of the country following the recent uprising.

Wednesday 12: The US TV host Bob Barker (*The Price is Right*) is born in Darrington, Washington.

Germany announces its gold reserves have been exhausted and it requires foreign loans.

Bob Barker is born on 12 December.

Thursday 13: Lord Alfred Douglas is sentenced to six months' imprisonment for libelling Winston Churchill over alleged stock market cheating.

Friday 14: US Prohibition agents announce they have stopped the 'rum leak' with a clampdown on alcohol smuggling from Canada and Britain.

Saturday 15: The theoretical physicist and mathematician Freeman Dyson is born in Crowthorne, Berkshire (died 2020).

Sunday 16: Mexican rebels capture the city of Cuautla.

Left: Georg Luger, inventor of the famous Luger automatic pistol (right) dies on 22 December.

Monday 17: The British government agrees to the setting up of the airline Imperial Airways, which goes into operation in April 1924.

Tuesday 18: France, Spain and Great Britain sign the Tangier Protocol which turns the Moroccan city into an international tax haven.

Wednesday 19: After refusing to abdicate, King George II of Greece is exiled to Romania.

The actor Gordon Jackson (*Upstairs, Downstairs, The Professionals*) is born in Glasgow (died 1990).

Thursday 20: The League of Nations begins an economic reconstruction programme for Hungary.

Friday 21: 50 people die in the worst aviation accident to this date, when the French airship *Dixmude* explodes over the Mediterranean Sea during a thunderstorm.

Great Britain grants independence to Nepal.

Saturday 22: Mexican rebels battle with government troops over control of the city of Puebla.

Gordon Jackson is born on 19 December.

December 1923

The formation of Imperial Airways is announced on 17 December.

The armaments designer Georg Luger dies aged 74.

Sunday 23: Mexican government troops put down the rebellion in Puebla.

Monday 24: The German Chancellor Wilhelm Marx states he is willing to pay war reparation providing 'unfair sanctions' against his country are removed.

An attempted communist coup in Spain is thwarted as organizers are arrested in Bilboa and Asturias.

Tuesday 25: The Oscar Hammerstein musical *Mary Jane McKane* opens on Broadway.

Wednesday 26: A major rescue operation to locate any survivors of the *Dixmude* airship crash on 21 December finds only one body, that of a crew member, off the Sicilian coast.

Left: Gustav Eiffel, designer of the Eiffel Tower, dies on 27 December.

Thursday 27: A failed assassination attempt takes place on Prince Regent Hirohito of Japan.

Gustav Eiffel, designer of France's Eiffel Tower, dies aged 91.

Friday 28: The George Bernard Shaw play *St Joan* opens at the Garrick Theatre, Manhattan.

Left: Clara Bow stars in *Black Oxen*, released on 29 December.

Saturday 29: The drama film *Black Oxen*, starring Clara Bow, is released.

Sunday 30: Major flooding occurs in Paris when the River Seine bursts its banks.

Mary Eaton stars in *Kid Boots*, which opens on 31 December.

Monday 31: The silent comedy star Fatty Arbuckle is divorced from actress Minta Durfee.

The Zeigfeld musical *Kid Boots* starring Eddie Cantor opens on Broadway.

Above: Mary Hay stars in the musical *Mary Jane McKane*, which opens on 25 December. Below: 'Fatty' Arbuckle is divorced on 31 December.

Other titles from Montpelier Publishing

A Little Book of Limericks:
Funny Rhymes for all the Family
ISBN 9781511524124

Scottish Jokes: A Wee Book of
Clean Caledonian Chuckles
ISBN 9781495297366

The Old Fashioned Joke Book:
Gags and Funny Stories
ISBN 9781514261989

Non-Religious Funeral Readings:
Philosophy and Poetry for Secular
Services
ISBN 9781500512835

Large Print Jokes: Hundreds of
Gags in Easy-to-Read Type
ISBN 9781517775780

**Spiritual Readings for Funerals
and Memorial Services**
ISBN 9781503379329

Victorian Murder: True Crimes,
Confessions and Executions
ISBN 9781530296194

Large Print Prayers: A Prayer for
Each Day of the Month
ISBN 9781523251476

**A Little Book of Ripping Riddles
and Confounding Conundrums**
ISBN 9781505548136

Vinegar uses: over 150 ways to use
vinegar
ISBN 9781512136623

Large Print Wordsearch:
100 Puzzles in Easy-to-Read Type
ISBN 9781517638894

The Pipe Smoker's Companion
ISBN 9781500441401

The Book of Church Jokes
ISBN 9781507620632

Bar Mitzvah Notebook
ISBN 9781976007781

Jewish Jokes
ISBN 9781514845769

Large Print Address Book
ISBN 9781539820031

How to Cook Without a Kitchen:
Easy, Healthy and Low-Cost Meals
9781515340188

Large Print Birthday Book
ISBN 9781544670720

Retirement Jokes
ISBN 9781519206350

Take my Wife: Hilarious Jokes of
Love and Marriage
ISBN 9781511790956

Welsh Jokes: A Little Book of
Wonderful Welsh Wit
ISBN 9781511612241

1001 Ways to Save Money: Thrifty
Tips for the Fabulously Frugal!
ISBN 9781505432534

Order online at Amazon or from your local bookshop

Printed in Great Britain
by Amazon

19224866R00037